Money Smart Children
Learn the
"Economic Law of Money Saving"

A Parent's Guide

Duke Coleman

Copyright © 2015 by Duke Coleman. 725700
Library of Congress Control Number: 2015916637

ISBN: Softcover   978-1-5144-1480-4
        Hardcover   978-1-5144-1481-1
        EBook   978-1-5144-1479-8

Print information available on the last page

Rev. date: 11/11/2015

To order additional copies of this book, contact:
Xlibris
1-888-795-4274
www.Xlibris.com
Orders@Xlibris.com

Money Smart Children

Learn the
"Economic Law of Money Saving"

A Parent's Guide

Duke Coleman

Story:

Balanced or Un-Balanced Money Economy, which one do you want?
Be careful how you answer before reading this story.

Beyond anyone's opinion, the "economic law of money saving" causes all money based economies to divide into two groups:

1) money rich "saving-people"; and 2) money poor "non-saving people".

You live within this law.

The economic law states: A money economy that allows people to save money for long periods of time will divide into one very small money-rich group and one very large money-poor group regardless of how hard people work or contribute to the money economy.

Following this law, an <u>un-balanced</u> money economy <u>allows everyone to save money</u> and accumulate as much as they want. But by saving and accumulating money the economy becomes un-balanced (see Figure-U below).

In contrast, a <u>balanced</u> money economy <u>does not allow anyone to save money</u> (for long times) and therefore does not allow anyone to accumulate unbalanced money. By not accumulating money the economy remains balanced because everyone spends their money (see Figure-B below).

To better understand the consequences of saving, imagine if the money economy consisted of $1,000,000,000. If 1,000,000,000 people all saved $1 everyone would be $1 money wealthy, but the economy would stop working because all the money would be stored and not spent.

If 1 person saved all $1,000,000,000 that person would be $1,000,000,000 wealthy and everyone else (999,999,999 people) would be $0 wealthy, (i.e., poor) and again the economy would stop because the money would be stored and not spent.

Somewhere between everyone owning all the money and one person owning all the money is where an un-balanced economy exists until the un-balanced process causes 1 person (or a small number of people) to accumulate and save all the money. This is why the money wealthy are getting richer and the money poor are getting poorer. Because we live in an un-balanced economy, it is critical that you save and accumulate money if you do not want to end up poor.

Remember in contrast, if no one was allowed to save money the economy would stay in balance and never stop.

This story is meant to motivate you (and/or your children) to take saving money very serious for your wellbeing. By sharing the reasons why this is true, I hope to illustrate the importance of saving in a way that leaves you with a strong desire to make wise choices with lasting benefits. The story starts by answering a few questions about how our existing un-balanced economy works to establish a frame of reference (a point of view). Then briefly for comparison we will explore what a balanced money economy would look like to know the difference. But then we will ignore the balanced economy because people are unlikely to ever adopt one for real because they could no longer store up money for long periods of time. After answering the questions, the points of the story are further described by using simple diagram models explaining "where money $ comes from" and "where money $ goes to" logically. Then with some simple math, one of the model diagrams is used to show "how mathematically quick" the money goes to people who save and away from people that do not. This reveals why it is so important to make good choices about saving to be money successful. Hopefully money will freely flow your way once you adopt these ideas.

Let us look at figure-U below and answer the following questions. Before the questions though, read the boxes (1), (2), & (3) and notice the arrows to see how money flows "out of balance" into the "saving-people box (3)".

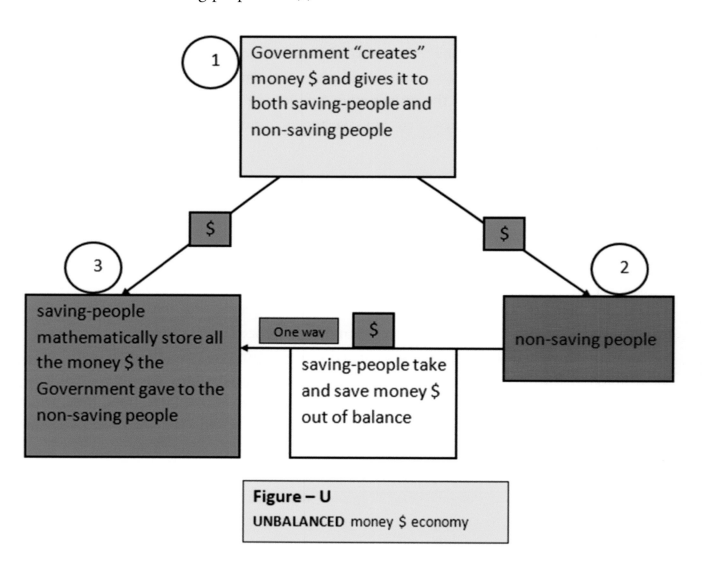

1) Government "creates" money $ and gives it to both saving-people and non-saving people

$

3) saving-people mathematically store all the money $ the Government gave to the non-saving people

One way $ saving-people take and save money $ out of balance

$

2) non-saving people

Figure – U
UNBALANCED money $ economy

Questions:

1. Where did money come from in the beginning?

   Answer: it was created out of nowhere by the Government Department (GD) to make trading goods and services easy and efficient. The GD gave the money to two groups, the saving-people group (SG) and the non-saving people group (NSG). Notice how all the money the GD creates always flows to the money-saving group (SG) in the end.

2. What would happen if the GD stopped creating money completely so only a fixed constant amount of money was available for people to use?

   Answer: the money "economy would stop". Once the saving-people took all the money away from the non-saving people, the money would get stuck with the money-saving group and stop. This means if people kept doing business long enough, only the people who saved money would have any in the end. *For full understanding think about what would happen as time went on if most of the "saving-people" converted over into "non-saving people". The economy would keep going until the last saving person ended up with all the money and then the economy would stop. But then, if the last saving-person finally agreed to be a non-saving person the economy would "balance" and continue working forever (see Figure-B below). (I would not bet on this happening though, so plan for living in an un-balanced economy for now).

3. Finally, imagine what would happen after the saving people took all the money and the economy stopped. Then what would happen if the GD started creating more money and giving the money to the non-saving people as fast as the money saving people were taking it?

   Answer: the money "economy would never stop". All the money being taken by the saving-people would first come from the GD, go to the non-saving people, and then to the saving-people. This is basically the way our economy works today and why there is so much money in the economy. This is why there will be a lot more money in the economy in the future and why you need to save to remain competitive.

In this story, you must realize there were wealthy and poor people before the Government Department (GD) invented and created this thing we call "money" out of nowhere. People had what we will call "human wealth" (e.g., food, water, clothes, housing, health, medicine, education, entertainment, vacation time, political power, etc.) that made them rich or poor. Realize "money rich" and "money poor" people were only created after the GD created the "money economy". Because money works very well for trading "human wealth" we now live in a "combined" money wealth and a human wealth economy that confuses the two kinds of wealth. (The "human wealth" economy will be described later in a future separate book for clarity.)

So, for this book recognize the story has intentionally separated out the "money economy" to highlight how it works by itself. First we consider how it works "logically" and then how it works "mathematically" through a simple example. Separating out the money economy removes confusion that hides the painful truth from many people that they are mathematically doomed to end up with a smaller and smaller portion of all the money if they do not learn to take and save money from the people around them. Because money-saving people are storing a larger and larger portion of the total money, non-saving people are becoming more "money poor". This story makes it clear why becoming "money poor" is the most likely result most people can expect even if they are responsible and hard-working in an "unbalanced" money economy. An obvious exception to this doom is that non-saving people that make a lot of money continuously from their job and/or business will always be "money wealthy". If they keep their job and/or business going for their whole life, they too will always have money. Your children should be aware of this option also. It is a good way to be competitive if they can make it work, but it is more difficult and less common as people get older.

At this point in the story (for reference) let us make a quick comparison with what it would be like to live in a "balanced" economy to see the difference (see figure-B below). Read the boxes and notice the arrows to see how money flows "in balance" between the two "non-saving people" boxes (2) and (3).

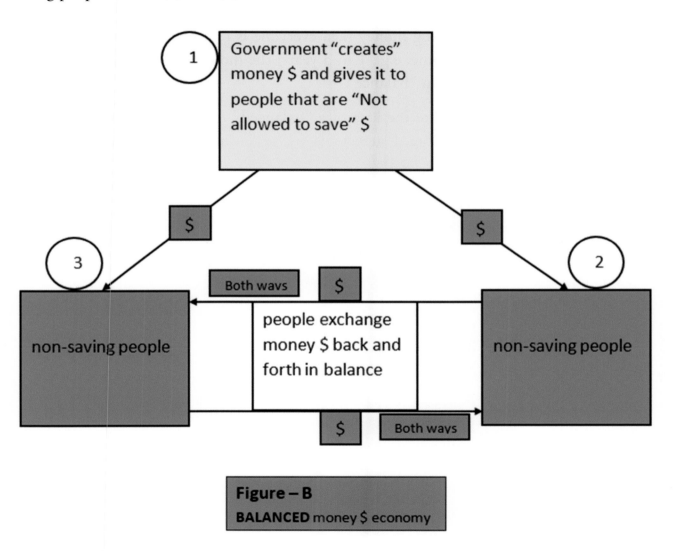

Figure – B
BALANCED money $ economy

If we lived in a "balanced" money economy, all the money created by the GD would in the same way (as an un-balanced economy) begin by flowing to the two groups of people, except now both groups would be non-saving people. Then notice how the "money" is forced to flow back a forth between the two groups because there is nowhere else for it to go. The money would not get stuck on one side in the "saving-people" group because no one would be allowed to save. By not saving money (i.e., everyone is required to spend their money within a sensible duration of time, e.g., 1 to 3 years) the money just flows back and forth and the money economy stays in "balance".

But recognize people do not like the idea of a "balanced" money economy because they are not allowed to save. Therefore, I suggest we ignore it and return our attention to the "unbalanced" situation.

Our "unbalanced" money economy is made up of three (3) main pieces (see figure-U repeated below).

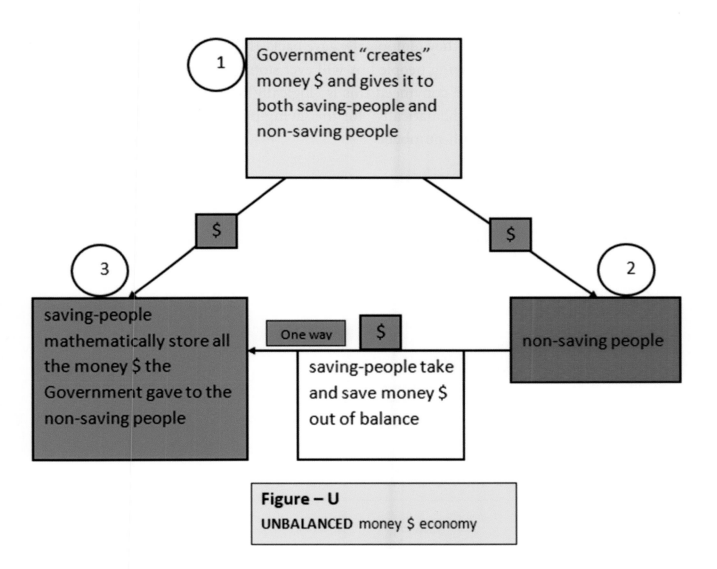

Figure – U
UNBALANCED money $ economy

Look at figure-U and be fully convinced all the money ever created eventually flows from the Government-(1) and non-saving people-(2) into the saving-people-(3) box. Even think about when the saving-people temporarily give back part of the money through purchases, taxes, paid out wages, etc. to the Government and non-saving people. Eventually the saving-people take back all the money they temporarily gave back. If this is not clear, try to imagine any possible way the money-saving people box will ever stop taking more and more money until it has it all. Once you are convinced this is "logically true" we can move on to look at how little time it takes "mathematically" for the saving-people to take all the money by exploring a simple example with numbers.

For this mathematical example we will call the "unbalanced" money economy Option-1 (see figure-1 below and notice words are replaced with abbreviations GD, SG, NSG for short).

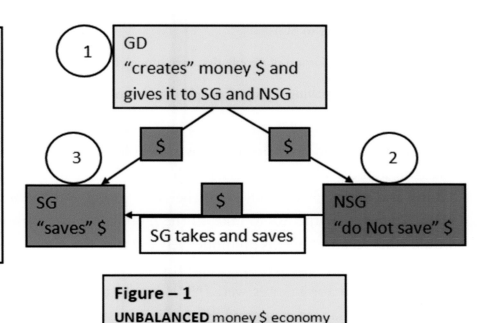

Option-1
How the money economy works and why the money-savers SG get mathematically money rich and non-savers NSG get mathematically money poor.

1 — GD "creates" money $ and gives it to SG and NSG

$

3 — SG "saves" $

$ — SG takes and saves

2 — NSG "do Not save" $

Figure – 1
UNBALANCED money $ economy

Review the meanings of the following abbreviations because they are used from here on.

Option-1 = the "unbalanced" money economy (Figure-1)

GD = the Government Department that creates money from nowhere any time it wants and gives it to the Saving Group (SG) & the Non-saving Group (NSG) to keep the money flowing "unbalanced" from GD & NSG to SG)

SG = the Saving Group of people that save money they take from GD & NSG

NSG = the Non-saving Group of people that do not save money they take from GD & SG

The example we consider is the following. Imagine a Government Department (GD) starts a new economy and gives both groups of people, (e.g., 100 SG people and 100 NSG people) the same amount of money to start with (e.g., $500 each). Next imagine the SG group starts taking and saving 3% money from the NSG group. With 3% savings you will see it takes about 23 years for the SG to take all the money. After that number of years, the economy would stop because there is no money left to take. Take note that if the savings were greater than 3% it would take less years and if the savings were less than 3% it would take more years. In fact, if the savings were 0% it would take forever (i.e., never stop, which is the meaning of a balanced economy). Recognize the story is created "mathematically simplified" to illustrate the point that in some short finite amount of time the 3% savings economy stops if the GD does not create and distribute more new money into the economy. This GD creating more money over and over again is an unavoidable part of choosing to create an "unbalanced" money economy.

So let us get back to the simple math example where the Government Department (GD) creates $1000 = $500 + $500 and gives it evenly to the SG & NSG groups, (i.e., each group begins with $500 each).

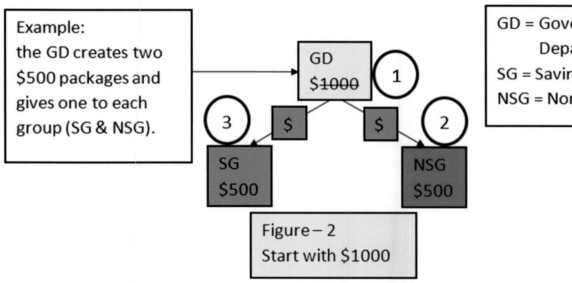

Example:
the GD creates two $500 packages and gives one to each group (SG & NSG).

GD
$1000

SG
$500

NSG
$500

Figure – 2
Start with $1000

GD = Government Department
SG = Saving-Group
NSG = Non-Saving Group

Now watch what happens mathematically when the SG people take and save 3% money from the NSG people each year, (i.e., notice it takes 23 years to take all the money).

After one (1) year the SG have taken $15 = [(1+3%)^1 * $500 -$500] and end with

$515 = [$500 + $15]. The NSG end with $485 = [$500 - $15].

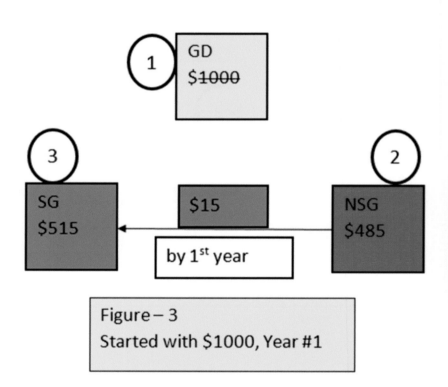

Year #1

The first year shows money moves in only one direction, from SG to NSG. This pattern continues.

Figure – 3
Started with $1000, Year #1

After ten (10) years the SG have taken $172 = [(1+3%)^{10} * \$500 - \$500]$ and end with $672 = [\$500 + \$172]$. The NSG end with $328 = [\$500 - \$172]$.

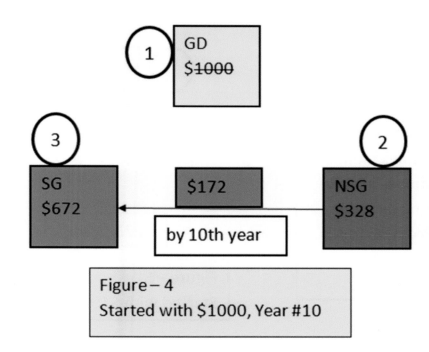

Year #10
The tenth year shows money moves in only one direction, from SG to NSG. This pattern continues.

Figure – 4
Started with $1000, Year #10

After twenty three (23) years the SG have taken $487 = [(1+3%)^23 * $500 - $500] and end with $987 = [$500 + $487]. The NSG end with $13 = [$500 - $487]. At this point in time, the SG now have approximately all the money.

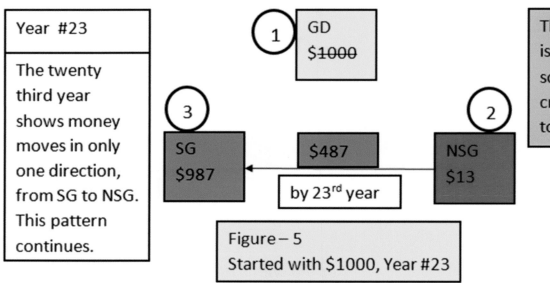

Year #23

The twenty third year shows money moves in only one direction, from SG to NSG. This pattern continues.

1 GD $~~1000~~

The money economy is just about to stop, so the GD needs to create more money to keep it working.

3 SG $987

$487

2 NSG $13

by 23rd year

Figure – 5
Started with $1000, Year #23

This table shows year by year how the money flows to SG from NSG over the first 23 years.

GD gives SG and NSG $500 each to start						
	Year	SG $$$	interest%	gain sum	NSG $	loss sum
	0	500.00			500.00	
start	1	500	3.00	515.00	500	485.00	start
	2	515.00	3.00	530.45	485.00	469.55
	3	530.45	3.00	546.36	469.55	453.64
	4	546.36	3.00	562.75	453.64	437.25
	5	562.75	3.00	579.64	437.25	420.36
	6	579.64	3.00	597.03	420.36	402.97
	7	597.03	3.00	614.94	402.97	385.06
	8	614.94	3.00	633.39	385.06	366.61
	9	633.39	3.00	652.39	366.61	347.61
	10	652.39	3.00	672	347.61	328
	11	671.96	3.00	692.12	328.04	307.88
	12	692.12	3.00	712.88	307.88	287.12
	13	712.88	3.00	734.27	287.12	265.73
	14	734.27	3.00	756.29	265.73	243.71
	15	756.29	3.00	778.98	243.71	221.02
	16	778.98	3.00	802.35	221.02	197.65
	17	802.35	3.00	826.42	197.65	173.58
	18	826.42	3.00	851.22	173.58	148.78
	19	851.22	3.00	876.75	148.78	123.25
	20	876.75	3.00	903.06	123.25	96.94
	21	903.06	3.00	930.15	96.94	69.85
	22	930.15	3.00	958.05	69.85	41.95
finish	23	958.05	3.00	987	41.95	13	finish

Table – 1
Start with $1000, years #1 - #23

Because the money economy is just about to stop, the Government Department (GD) needs to create and distribute more new money to keep it working. So that is what it does. More money is created and distributed to each group (for example $1000 = $500 for SG + $500 for NSG).

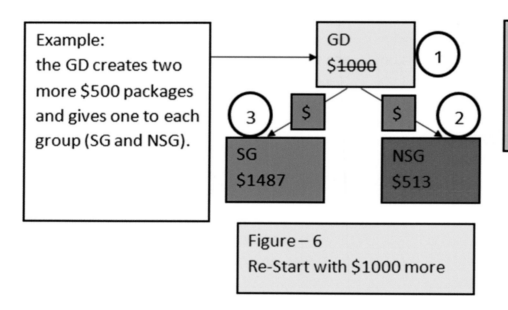

Example:
the GD creates two more $500 packages and gives one to each group (SG and NSG).

GD
$1000

1

3

$

$

2

SG
$1487

NSG
$513

Now each group has more money, but there is a problem with how little time it will last.

Figure – 6
Re-Start with $1000 more

But notice in this step a problem arises that must be fixed. Because the SG people now start the next saving cycle with a larger portion of all the money ($1487 = $987 + $500) than the NSG people ($513 = $13 + $500), the next saving time decreases from 23 years down to 10 years (a much smaller amount of time). This means the "unbalanced" money economy will begin to stop this time in only 10 years because of the new mathematical situation.

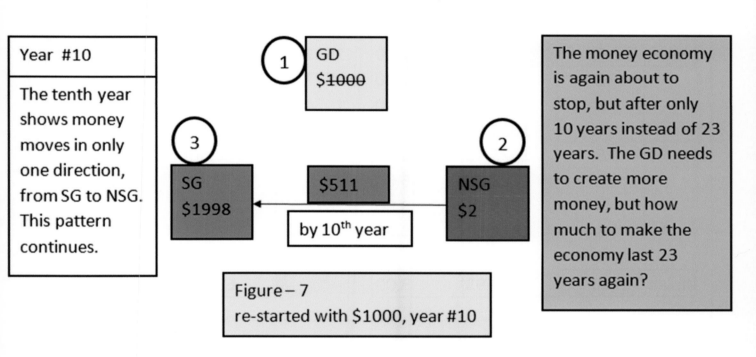

Year #10

The tenth year shows money moves in only one direction, from SG to NSG. This pattern continues.

① GD $~~1000~~

③ SG $1998

$511
by 10th year

② NSG $2

The money economy is again about to stop, but after only 10 years instead of 23 years. The GD needs to create more money, but how much to make the economy last 23 years again?

Figure – 7
re-started with $1000, year #10

This table shows year by year how the money flows to SG from NSG over the next 10 years.

	Year	SG $$$	interest%	gain sum	NSG $	loss sum	
	\multicolumn	GD gives SG and NSG $500 more each to restart					
	0	500.00			500.00		
start	1	1487	3.00	1531.40	513	468.60	start
	2	1531.40	3.00	1577.34	468.60	422.66	
	3	1577.34	3.00	1624.66	422.66	375.34	
	4	1624.66	3.00	1673.40	375.34	326.60	
	5	1673.40	3.00	1723.60	326.60	276.40	
	6	1723.60	3.00	1775.31	276.40	224.69	
	7	1775.31	3.00	1828.57	224.69	171.43	
	8	1828.57	3.00	1883.43	171.43	116.57	
	9	1883.43	3.00	1939.93	116.57	60.07	
finish	10	1939.93	3.00	1998	60.07	2	finish

Table – 2
re-started with $1000 more, years #1 - #10

In other words, the greater portion of all the money the SG restarts with, the shorter time it takes SG to take all the NSG money. To adjust for this problem and cause the money savings time to be 23 years again, the GS can simply create and distribute more than $500 to each group. Specifically, if the GD creates $36,000 for each group ($72,000 total = $36,000 SG + $36,000 NSG), then the next saving cycle time will return to 23 years. The SG people now restart the next saving cycle with about the same proportion of all the money ($36987 = $987 + $36000) as the NSG people ($36013 = $13 + $36000) and the money economy continues to work for another good long time (i.e., 23 more years).

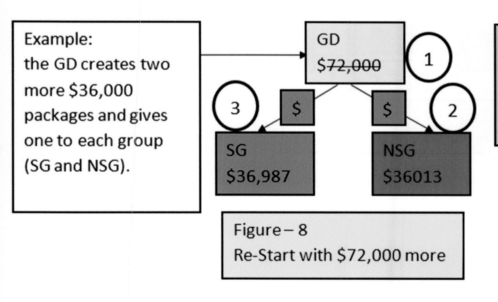

Example:
the GD creates two more $36,000 packages and gives one to each group (SG and NSG).

Now each group restarts with about the same proportion of money for another 23 years.

Figure – 8
Re-Start with $72,000 more

After twenty three (23) more years the SG have taken $36,010 = [(1+3%)^23 * $36,987 - $36,987] and end with $72,997 = [$36987 + $36,010]. The NSG end with $3 = [$36,013 - $36,010]. At this point in time, the SG now have approximately all the money again.

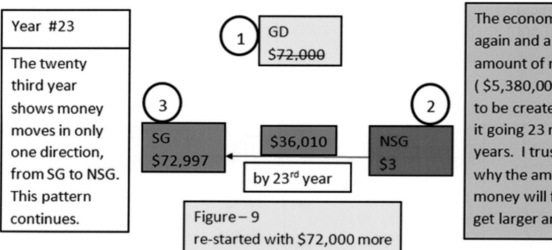

Year #23

The twenty third year shows money moves in only one direction, from SG to NSG. This pattern continues.

1 GD $72,000

3

SG $72,997

$36,010

by 23rd year

2

NSG $3

The economy stops again and a greater amount of money ($5,380,000) needs to be created to keep it going 23 more years. I trust you see why the amount of money will forever get larger and larger.

Figure – 9
re-started with $72,000 more

This table shows year by year how the money flows to SG from NSG over 23 more years.

	GD gives SG and NSG $36,000 more each to restart						
	Year	SG $$$	interest%	gain sum	NSG $	loss sum	
	0	36000.00			36000.00		
start	1	36987	3.00	38096.40	36013	34903.60	start
	2	38096.40	3.00	39239.29	34903.60	33760.71	
	3	39239.29	3.00	40416.47	33760.71	32583.53	
	4	40416.47	3.00	41628.96	32583.53	31371.04	
	5	41628.96	3.00	42877.83	31371.04	30122.17	
	6	42877.83	3.00	44164.17	30122.17	28835.83	
	7	44164.17	3.00	45489.09	28835.83	27510.91	
	8	45489.09	3.00	46853.76	27510.91	26146.24	
	9	46853.76	3.00	48259.38	26146.24	24740.62	
	10	48259.38	3.00	49707.16	24740.62	23292.84	
	11	49707.16	3.00	51198.37	23292.84	21801.63	
	12	51198.37	3.00	52734.32	21801.63	20265.68	
	13	52734.32	3.00	54316.35	20265.68	18683.65	
	14	54316.35	3.00	55945.84	18683.65	17054.16	
	15	55945.84	3.00	57624.22	17054.16	15375.78	
	16	57624.22	3.00	59352.95	15375.78	13647.05	
	17	59352.95	3.00	61133.53	13647.05	11866.47	
	18	61133.53	3.00	62967.54	11866.47	10032.46	
	19	62967.54	3.00	64856.57	10032.46	8143.43	
	20	64856.57	3.00	66802.26	8143.43	6197.74	
	21	66802.26	3.00	68806.33	6197.74	4193.67	
	22	68806.33	3.00	70870.52	4193.67	2129.48	
finish	23	70870.52	3.00	72997	2129.48	3	finish

Table – 3
re-started with $72,000 more, years #1 - #23

Notice the economy stops again though, and now the GD needs to create $5,380,000 total = $2,690,500 SG + $2,690,500 NSG to restart the economy for 23 more years. I trust you now see why the amount of money in the economy will forever get larger and larger.

This table shows year by year how the money flows to SG from NSG over 23 more years.

GD gives SG and NSG $2,690,500 more each to restart						
	Year	SG $$$	interest%	gain sum	NSG $	loss sum
	0	2690500			2690500	
start	1	2763497	3.00	2846402	2690503	2607598	start
	2	2846402	3.00	2931794	2607598	2522206
	3	2931794	3.00	3019747	2522206	2434253
	4	3019747	3.00	3110340	2434253	2343660
	5	3110340	3.00	3203650	2343660	2250350
	6	3203650	3.00	3299760	2250350	2154240
	7	3299760	3.00	3398752	2154240	2055248
	8	3398752	3.00	3500715	2055248	1953285
	9	3500715	3.00	3605736	1953285	1848264
	10	3605736	3.00	3713908	1848264	1740092
	11	3713908	3.00	3825326	1740092	1628674
	12	3825326	3.00	3940085	1628674	1513915
	13	3940085	3.00	4058288	1513915	1395712
	14	4058288	3.00	4180037	1395712	1273963
	15	4180037	3.00	4305438	1273963	1148562
	16	4305438	3.00	4434601	1148562	1019399
	17	4434601	3.00	4567639	1019399	886361
	18	4567639	3.00	4704668	886361	749332
	19	4704668	3.00	4845808	749332	608192
	20	4845808	3.00	4991182	608192	462818
	21	4991182	3.00	5140918	462818	313082
	22	5140918	3.00	5295145	313082	158855
finish	23	5295145	3.00	5454000	158855	0.32	finish

Table – 4
re-started with $5,381,000 more, years #1 - #23

So the pattern repeats over and over, which keeps the "<u>unbalanced</u>" money economy working. Notice, giving the NSG people more and more money is the key to keeping it going. Remember, if the GD ever stops giving money to the NSG it will stop. Notice also, if the GD even starts giving the NSG money slower than the SG are taking it the economy will stop. But if the GD gives the NSG money as quick or quicker than the SG takes it, then the pattern can mathematically continue forever.

Although as you can guess. The amount of money in the economy after many years becomes excessively large. This is why we have trillions of dollars in the economy now. The money economy started out small, but requires an enormous amount of money be continually created out of nowhere and added to it. Overall, by the GD creating and distributing the right amount of money, the SG continues to save at the same time the NSG gets just enough to keep giving it to the SG. Both groups remain much happier than if the GD stops creating money. Mostly this story shows that what you buy in the future is going to require a lot more money than it does now. You may have to pay a hundred dollars for a loaf of bread someday, but the bread will be just as tasty.

I hope now it is obvious to you and your children why they need to work hard, save, invest, and take money from the people around them to stay money ahead in the future. I hope the story makes the follow list of important points clear:

1. most people want an "unbalanced money economy" (because they want the freedom to save money which causes the "unbalance")

2. logically "the portion of all the money" created by the Government Department always continues to get larger and larger with "money-saving people" and to get smaller and smaller with "money non-saving people"

3. a "balanced money economy" could stop the unbalanced result, but people will never agree to create a balanced economy, so you need to learn to save to compete

4. the more money the saving-people save, the faster they take money from people that do not save (e.g., compare taking 3% of $500 = $15, with 3% of $2,690,500 = $88,815 to image how fast)

5. no matter how little "human wealth building work" money-saving people do, an unbalanced money economy continues to give them a larger portion of the money. They get and save more money just by owning and loaning money

6. no matter how much "human wealth building work" money non-saving people do, an unbalanced money economy continues to leave them with a smaller portion of the total available money

7. the faster the money-saving people save money, the faster the Government Department has to create more money to keep the money economy working

8. the amount of money the Government Department will create for the future unbalanced economy will be larger and larger with no end to the increase

9. the amount of money your children will need to buy things in their future will be much larger than it is today so they need to learn how to get and save money

Simple logic and math were used to make these points. There may be people that say some of these points are not true, but will fail to explain why. They may try to convince you and your children that these logical and mathematically clear items are not true because the money economy is much more complex. Actually it is not. The unbalanced economy is mathematically designed to make money-saving people get a larger and larger portion of the money over time. Money-saving people cause the Government to keep creating more money out of nowhere and give it to the non-saving people. Then the saving-people take it from the non-saving people which increases the saving people's proportion. The money economy is unbalanced by design and so in time you and your children will see a small portion of money-saving people get very money wealthy while a lot of non-saving hard working people will end up money poor. This story should convince you there is no other likely outcome for your lives. You need to learn how to take, save, and invest money well to provide for yourself and family.

Remember, it is the people's choice to create a money based economy that allows people to save money for as long as they want (i.e., the choice to have an "un-balanced money economy"). So now that we have it, stop wasting your time trying to fix money inequality by making things fair and balanced. Just vote for a Government that creates money faster than people save it and save as much as you can. Everything will keep working fine if this continues. The "economic law of money saving" will keep you going. Good luck!

Printed in the United States
By Bookmasters